D1810771

THE FACTS ON
ABORTION

John Ankerberg
& John Weldon

HARVEST HOUSE PUBLISHERS
Eugene, Oregon 97402

Except where otherwise indicated, all Scripture quotations in this book are taken from the New American Standard Bible, © 1960, 1962, 1963, 1968, 1971, 1972, 1973, 1975, 1977 by The Lockman Foundation. Used by permission.

Verses marked NIV are taken from the Holy Bible, New International Version®. Copyright © 1973, 1978, 1984 by the International Bible Society. Used by permission of Zondervan Publishing House. The "NIV" and "New International Version" trademarks are registered in the United States Patent and Trademark Office by International Bible Society.

Other books by
John Ankerberg and John Weldon

The Facts on Abortion
The Facts on Angels
The Facts on Astrology
The Facts on Creation vs. Evolution
The Facts on the Faith Movement
The Facts on False Teaching in the Church
The Facts on Hinduism
The Facts on Holistic Health and the New Medicine
The Facts on Homosexuality
The Facts on Islam
The Facts on the Jehovah's Witnesses
The Facts on Jesus the Messiah
The Facts on Life After Death
The Facts on the Masonic Lodge
The Facts on the Mind Sciences
The Facts on the Mormon Church
The Facts on the New Age Movement
The Facts on the Occult
The Facts on Rock Music
The Facts on Roman Catholicism
The Facts on Self-Esteem, Psychology and the Recovery Movement
The Facts on Sex Education
The Facts on Spirit Guides
The Facts on UFOs and Other Supernatural Phenomena

THE FACTS ON ABORTION

Copyright © 1995 by the Ankerberg Theological
Research Institute
Published by Harvest House Publishers
Eugene, Oregon 97402

ISBN 1-56507-353-3

Printed in the United States of America.

95 96 97 98 99 00 — 10 9 8 7 6 5 4 3 2 1

CONTENTS

Preface

Preface

"The most dangerous place in the world is in the womb."

—*Cardinal Sin of the Philippines*[1]

"The fact that abortion and infanticide result in the destruction of innocent human beings cannot, in itself, be a reason for viewing such actions as wrong."

—*Michael Tooley*[2]

"Although every holocaust ever perpetrated is an unprecedented event in its own right, this should not detract from what all holocausts share in common . . . the systematic and widespread destruction of millions looked upon as indiscriminate masses of sub-human expendables.

"The cultural environment for a human holocaust is present whenever any society can be misled into defining individuals as less than human and therefore devoid of value and respect."

—*William Brennan*[3]

"Mental defectives do not have a right to life, and therefore might be killed for food—if we should develop a taste for human flesh—or for the purpose of scientific experimentation."

—*Peter Singer*[4]

American Deaths

Based on current figures, by the year 2000 we will be approaching 50 million abortions in the United States alone. In a short 27 years (1973–2000), we will have aborted *30 times* the number of Americans lost in all U.S. wars.

In the table following, the war casualties represent rounded figures for all American combat and combat-related deaths.

American Deaths Resulting from War and Abortion
(Each cross represents 100,000 deaths)

Revolutionary War (25,000)   -
Civil War (600,000)   † † † † † †
World War I (120,000)   †
World War II (600,000)   † † † † † †
Korean War (55,000)   -
Vietnam War (56,000)   -
Modern Abortion Deaths   † † † † † † † † † † † † † † † † † † †
     † † † † † † † † † † † † † † † † † † †
     † † † † † † † † † † † † † † † † † † †
1973–90   † † † † † † † † † † † † † † † † † † †
(25,200,000)   † † † † † † † † † † † † † † † † † † †
     † † † † † † † † † † † † † † † † † † †
     † † † † † † † † † † † † † † † † † † †
     † † † † † † † † † † † † † † † † † † †
     † † † † † † † † † † † † † † † † † † †
     † † † † † † † † † † † † † † † † † † †
     † † † † † † † † † † † † † † † † † † †
     † † † † † † † † † † † † † † † † † † †
     † † † † † † † † † † † † † † † † † † †
     † † † † † † † † † † † † † † † † † † †

to A.D. 2000   † † † † † † † † † † † † † † † † † † †
(48,000,000 estimated)   † † † † † † † † † † † † † † † † † † †

Worldwide, the abortion toll may approach one *billion* dead: 20 times the American estimate.[5]

1. What does modern science conclude about when human life begins?

Many people mistakenly feel that abortion is a "religious" issue. But it is not. It is a scientific issue and, specifically, a biological issue. The scientific authorities on when life begins are biologists. But these are often the last people consulted in seeking an answer to the question. What modern science has concluded is crystal clear: Human life begins at conception. This is a matter of scientific *fact*, not philosophy, speculation, opinion, conjecture, or theory. Today, the evidence that human life begins at conception is a fact so well documented that no intellectually honest and informed scientist or physician can deny it.

In 1973, the Supreme Court concluded in its *Roe v. Wade* decision that it did not have to decide the "difficult question" of when life begins. Why? In essence, they said, "It is impossible to say when human life begins."[6] The Court misled the public then, and others continue to mislead the public today.

Anyone familiar with recent Supreme Court history knows that two years before *Roe v. Wade*, in October 1971, a group of 220 distinguished physicians, scientists, and professors submitted an *amicus curiae* brief (advice to a court on some legal matter) to the Supreme Court. They showed the Court how modern science had already established that human life is a continuum and that the unborn child from the moment of conception on is a person and must be considered a person, like its mother.[7] The brief set as its task "to show how clearly and conclusively modern science—embryology, fetology, genetics, perinatology, all of biology—establishes the humanity of the unborn child."[8] For example, "In its seventh week, [the pre-born child] bears the familiar external features and all the internal organs of the adult. . . . The brain in configuration is already like the adult brain and sends out impulses that coordinate the function of other organs. . . . The heart beats sturdily. The stomach produces digestive juices. The liver manufactures blood cells and the kidneys begin to function by extracting uric acid from the child's blood. . . . The muscles of the arms and body can already be set in motion. After the eighth week . . . *everything* is already present that will be found in the full term baby."[9] This brief proved beyond any doubt scientifically that human life begins at conception and that "the unborn is a person within the meaning of the Fifth and Fourteenth Amendments."[10]

In fact, *prior* to *Roe v. Wade*, nearly every medical and biological textbook assumed or taught that human life begins at conception. That human life begins at conception was an accepted medical fact, but not necessarily a discussed medical fact. This is why many textbooks did not devote a discussion to this issue. But many others did. For example, Mr. Patrick A. Trueman helped prepare a 1975 brief before the Illinois Supreme Court on the unborn child. He noted,

> We introduced an affidavit from a professor of medicine detailing 19 textbooks on the subject of embryology used in medical schools today which universally agreed that human life begins at conception . . . those textbooks agree that is when human life begins. The court didn't strike that down—the court couldn't strike that down because there was a logical/biological basis for that law.[11]

Thus, even though the Supreme Court had been properly informed as to the scientific evidence, they still chose to argue that the evidence was insufficient to show the pre-born child was fully human. In essence, their decision merely reflected social engineering and opinion, not scientific fact. Even during the growing abortion debate in 1970, the editors of the scientific journal *California Medicine* noted the "curious avoidance of the scientific fact, which everyone really knows, that human life begins at conception and is continuous whether intra- or extra-uterine until death."[12]

Even 25 years after the abortion revolution that politicized scientific opinion, medical texts today still often assume or affirm that human life begins at conception. For example, Keith L. Moore is professor and chairman of the Department of Anatomy at the University of Toronto Faculty of Medicine. His text, *The Developing*

Human: Clinically Oriented Embryology, is widely used in core courses in medical embryology. This text asserts:

> The processes by which a child develops from a single cell are *miraculous.* . . .
> *Human development is a continuous process that begins when an ovum from a female is fertilized by a sperm from a male.* Growth and differentiation transform the *zygote,* a single cell . . . into a multicellular adult human being.[13]

The reference to the "miraculous processes" in a purely secular text is not surprising. Even a single strand of DNA from a human cell contains information equivalent to a library of 1,000 volumes. The complexity of the zygote itself according to Dr. Hymie Gordon, chief geneticist at the Mayo Clinic, "is so great that it is beyond our comprehension."[14] In a short nine months' time, one fertilized ovum grows into 6,000 million cells that become a living, breathing person.

Further, medical dictionaries and encyclopedias all affirm that the embryo is human. Among many we could cite are *Dorland's Illustrated Medical Dictionary, Tuber's Cyclopedic Medical Dictionary,* and the *Encyclopedia and Dictionary of Medicine, Nursing and Allied Health* which defines the embryo as "the human young from the time of fertilization of the ovum until the beginning of the third month."[15]

In 1981, the United States Congress conducted hearings to answer the question, "When does human life begin?" A group of internationally known scientists appeared before a Senate judiciary subcommittee.[16] The U.S. Congress was told by Harvard University Medical School's Professor Micheline Matthews-Roth, "In biology and in medicine, it is an accepted fact that the life of any individual organism reproducing by sexual reproduction begins at conception. . . ."[17]

Dr. Watson A. Bowes, Jr., of the University of Colorado Medical School, testified that "the beginning of a single human life is from a biological point of view a simple and straightforward matter—the beginning is conception. This straightforward biological fact should not be distorted to serve sociological, political or economic goals."[18]

Dr. Alfred Bongiovanni of the University of Pennsylvania Medical School noted: "The standard medical texts have long taught that human life begins at conception."[19]

He added: "I am no more prepared to say that these early stages represent an incomplete human being than I would be to say that the child prior to the dramatic effects of puberty . . . is not a human being. This is human life at every stage albeit incomplete until late adolescence."[20]

Dr. McCarthy De Mere, who is a practicing physician as well as a law professor at the University of Tennessee, testified: "The exact moment of the beginning [of] personhood and of the human body is at the moment of conception."[21]

World-famous geneticist Dr. Jerome Lejeune, professor of fundamental genetics at the University of Descarte, Paris, France, declared, "each individual has a very unique beginning, the moment of its conception."[22]

Dr. Lejeune also emphasized: "The human nature of the human being from conception to old age is not a metaphysical contention, it is plain experimental evidence."[23]

The chairman of the Department of Medical Genetics at the Mayo Clinic, Professor Hymie Gordon, testified, "By all the criteria of modern molecular biology, life is present from the moment of conception."[24]

He further emphasized: "now we can say, unequivocally, that the question of when life begins . . . is an established scientific fact. . . . It is an established fact that all life, including human life, begins at the moment of conception."[25]

At that time the U.S. Senate proposed Senate Bill 158, called the "Human Life Bill." These hearings, which lasted eight days, involving 57 witnesses, were conducted by Senator John East. This Senate report concluded:

> Physicians, biologists, and other scientists agree that conception marks the beginning of the life of a human being—a being that is alive and is a member of the human species. There

is overwhelming agreement on this point in countless medical, biological, and scientific writings.[26]

In 1981, only a single scientist disagreed with the majority's conclusion, and he did so on philosophical rather than scientific grounds. In fact, abortion advocates, although invited to do so, failed to produce even one expert witness who would specifically testify that life begins at any other point than conception.[27*]

Many other biologists and scientists agree that life begins at conception. All agree that there is no point of time or interval of time between conception and birth when the unborn is anything but human.

Professor Roth of Harvard University Medical School has emphasized, "It is incorrect to say that the biological data cannot be decisive. . . . It is scientifically correct to say that an individual human life begins at conception, when the egg and sperm join to form the zygote, and that this developing human always is a member of our species in all stages of its life."[28]

In conclusion, we agree with pioneer medical researcher, Landrum B. Shettles, M.D., Ph.D., that, "There is one fact that *no one can deny*; human beings begin at conception."[29]

Again, let us stress that this is *not* a matter of *religion*, it *is* solely a matter of *science*. Scientists of every religious view and no religious view—agnostic, Jewish, Buddhist, atheist, Christian, Hindu, etc.—all agree that life begins at conception. This explains why, for example, the International Code of Medical Ethics asserts: "A doctor must always bear in mind the importance of preserving human life from the time of conception until death."[30]

This is also why the Declaration of Geneva holds physicians to the following: "I will maintain the utmost respect for human life from the time of conception; even under threat, I will not use my medical knowledge contrary to the laws of humanity."[31] These statements can be found in the *World Medical Association Bulletin* for

---

*A few held that life may begin at implantation. However, implantation, while important, in no way defines life.

April 1949 (vol. 1, p. 22) and January 1950 (vol. 2, p. 5). In 1970, the World Medical Association again reaffirmed the Declaration of Geneva.[32]

What difference does it make that human life begins at conception? The difference is this: If human life begins at conception, then abortion is the killing of a human life.

To deny this fact is scientifically impossible.*

2. How has modern technology shown that human life begins at conception?

Recent developments of medical technology such as sound imaging and fetoscopy have permitted us to look into the womb and observe fetal development even from the point of conception. In terms of what we knew before, the difference is like observing a person's reflection in a pond compared to observing his reflection in a mirror. Modern fetology has given us an amazing and incredible look at the growth of the tiny individual in the mother's womb.[33]

Dr. Bernard Nathanson discusses how advances in modern technology caused him to radically alter his pro-abortion beliefs. Once known as "the abortion king" because of his prominence in the field and his presiding over 60,000 abortions,[34] he is today a vocal opponent of abortion because recent scientific advances in fetology forced him to accept the fact that the fetus was really a living human being:

> Ultrasound technology has been really the apparatus which has put the window in the womb. This was the first time we really could see the baby. Up till that time we never could. I mean, X-rays were static. You couldn't really use X-rays to prove or disprove much of anything about the fetus. But ultrasound gives us these very clear, precise pictures, allows us

---

*But to accept this fact and maintain that taking human life is not morally wrong is incredible. It is even reminiscent of Nazi Germany and yet today such arguments are increasingly accepted (e.g. *Biomedical Ethics and the Law* by James M. Humber and Robert F. Almeder, page 16; cf note 3).

to stimulate the child, see how it breathes, see how it moves, see how it swallows, see how it urinates, see how everything happens.

Now, there's been a new advance in this ultrasound technology which is known as transvaginal sonography. It's very exciting. [Before] the pictures were great, but they don't compare to these pictures—it's valuable for very early pregnancies.

We can see the gestational sac—the little sac of the pregnancy at two weeks following fertilization now with transvaginal sonography. [We] can see the heart beginning to beat at around 3 [to] 3-1/2 weeks now. So this has pushed back or updated a great many of our data about the unborn baby.

And I don't doubt that there are new technologies coming even now; for example, color ultrasound which is going to give us even clearer, more vivid pictures and increase our knowledge about the unborn patient here.[35]

The reason why modern science has come to the conclusion that human life begins at conception is because sound imaging and modern fetology have supported this judgment dramatically.[36] Every scientific law known (e.g., biogenesis—that is, life comes only from life) and every scientific fact (e.g., at conception a genetically new and unique human individual exists) demands this conclusion.

All of this is why the origin of human life cannot be defined at any other point (e.g., viability) than conception.

3. Isn't the fetus merely part of the mother's body?

Biologically, it is a scientific fact that in pregnancy there are two different bodies. First, there is the body of the woman. Second, there is another body—that of the child.

Evidence that there are two separate bodies can be seen from the fact that many women carry babies whose blood type differs from their own. It is medically impossible for a single individual to have two completely different blood types. Another illustration is that a female may be carrying in her womb a male child. This is clearly another body.

In addition, the body of the mother herself recognizes the child as a foreign body. This child would actually be rejected as "foreign tissue" by the woman's body were it not for the protection of the placenta. Doctors tell us that the placenta does not exist until, by its own development, the unborn child triggers the existence of the placenta and places it under his or her own power for self-preservation. In fact, the zygote actually begins to form the placenta within 72 hours.

Professor A. W. Liley, research professor in fetal physiology in Auckland, New Zealand, is known as the "Father of Fetology." He has stated,

> The fetus is not a passive, dependent, nerveless, fragile vegetable, as tradition has held, but a young human being, dynamic, plastic, resilient and in very large measure in charge of his environment and destiny. . . .
>
> In summary, the fetus organizes his mother . . . so that nutrients are deflected for fetal needs. . . .
>
> Throughout pregnancy it is the mother, not the fetus, who is passive and dependent.[37]

And,

> It is the embryo who stops his mother's periods and makes her womb habitable by developing a placenta and a protective capsule of fluid for himself. He regulates his own amniotic fluid volume and although women speak of their waters breaking or their membranes rupturing, these structures belong to the fetus. And finally, it is the fetus, not the mother, who decides when labor should be initiated.[38]

He has also stated, "Biologically, at no stage can we subscribe to the view that the fetus is a mere appendage of the mother. Genetically, mother and baby are separate individuals from conception. Physiologically, we must accept that the conceptus is, in a very large measure, in charge of the pregnancy."[39]

Further, it is a scientific fact that the little being in the womb has fingerprints, hands, feet, skin, eyes, ears, and genitals that are not the mother's. It has its own lungs, respiration, blood, heart, and circulation that are not the mother's. It has its own mouth, stomach, and digestion that are not the mother's.

Thus, the fetus is no more a part of the mother's body "than a nursing baby is part of her mother's breast or a test tube baby is part of a petri dish. So distinct is an embryo from a mother's womb that if a fertilized ovum from a black couple is transplanted into a white mother, she will have a black baby."[40]

In light of these undeniable scientific facts, we may now analyze the leading slogan of those arguing for abortion. Pro-choice advocates argue, "Every woman has the right to control her own body."

Every woman does have the right to control her own body, but she does not have the right to control the destiny of another human being—the baby in her womb. Let's examine the words used in the slogan.[41]

Every woman—At least 50 percent of the babies that are aborted are female human beings. Obviously, then, this slogan is not true for all of these aborted females. If they are part of what is termed "every woman," then obviously they haven't been given the right to control their own body. In fact, this slogan advocates the elitism of the powerful over the powerless rather than equality for all women. If all the aborted *women* could return to life, do you think they would agree that abortion is a practice that insures the rights and equality of *all* women?

Has the right—Legally, no one has absolute rights over other people. Human life is interrelated in such a way that many individual rights are necessarily curtailed for the welfare of society. For example, no female or male has the absolute right over his or her own body to mutilate it, to abuse it with drugs, to commit suicide, or to endanger the life of others. The same is true concerning human life in the womb. No one has the right to destroy it.

To control—To be "in control" involves the assuming of personal responsibility. But, in fact, it is largely *irresponsible actions* (e.g., promiscuity) that have led to most pregnancies. Abortion has thus become the convenient means to protect an immoral lifestyle, to cover over irresponsibility in birth control, or to escape the personal responsibility of child-rearing.

Her own body—As has already been demonstrated, the fetus is not the mother's body. It is an independent person with its own body. This is why Daniel Callahan, director of the Institute of Society, Ethics and the Life Sciences, has stated, "Genetically, hormonally, and in all organic respects save for the source of its nourishment, a fetus and even an embryo is separate from the woman."[42]

4. How can the embryo-fetus be a person? Isn't it just a "potential" person?

Abortionists claim that the living human fetus in the womb is not a full person, only a *potential* person. As such, it is not entitled to Constitutional protection as a human being and may be terminated by abortion.

In *Roe v. Wade* the Supreme Court arbitrarily implied that personhood only existed when the unborn fetus "presumably has the capability of meaningful life outside the mother's womb."[43] They ruled that "the word 'person' as used in the Fourteenth Amendment does not include the unborn."[44]

What is wrong with the Court's ruling that the fetus is a person only if it can exist outside the mother's womb in a "meaningful" way? What is wrong is that nowhere is "meaningful" defined. Meaningful life to one person may be denied by someone else. Who is to judge? As Richard Exley has written,

> If we base our decision on the prevailing pro-abortion rhetoric, then the unborn baby is not a person unless it is wanted by the mother—unless it is perfectly healthy, free from any deformity or other abnormality.
>
> The problem with that kind of reasoning is that it is based on the subjective opinion of a biased party—namely, the mother and/or the

abortionist. Not only does this approach deny the unborn their constitutional rights, it also opens a Pandora's box of potential abuses.[45]

So why must it be assumed that personhood begins at conception? First, because it is a scientific fact that *human life* begins at conception. Second, because every single "indicator" of personhood is not universally applicable, such as communication skill and level of consciousness or ability. These may be lacking in the pre-born, but so are they in many other *persons* with impairment or disease. Third, because human life and *human personhood* cannot be separated.[46]

How do dictionaries define the word *person*? The *Oxford American Dictionary* defines *person* as "an individual human being." *Webster's Third International Dictionary of the English Language* defines person as "an individual human being." In other words, once you have established (as we saw) that the zygote (the fertilized egg) is "an individual human being," you have also established that it *is a person*. The objective definition of personhood is the dictionary definition, but this is also the biological definition—"an individual human being." Thus, "by objective and scientific criteria, the individual *is a person throughout his entire biological development*."[47]

Why then is there so much confusion today over the issue of whether or not the fetus is a person? It is largely because many people have confused the term *personality* with *person*. *Personality* must be distinguished from *personhood*, since they are not equivalent:

> Personality is a psychological concept; personhood is an ontological [property and knowledge of being] category. Personality is a property, but personhood is the substance of being human. Personalities are formed by their surroundings, but personhood is created by God. Thus, personality is developed gradually, but personhood comes instantly at conception.[48]

Thus, to claim that a human being is not necessarily a

person is false. The distinction between "human being" and "person" is arbitrary. *No essential* differences exist between "being human" and "being a person."[49]

Thus, when human life is present, personhood is present and entitled to full human rights. These rights should never be denied by those who make arbitrary definitions concerning personhood.

Personhood and humanity do not grow; they are inherent. They are not something acquired; they are innate. No human being is "more" human than another.

These statements indicate the zygote-fetus is not a *potential* person because 1) it *is* alive (not potentially alive), because 2) it has a unique human nature (not a potential human nature), and because 3) at any stage of development it is most accurately described as an actual person with great potential. From zygote on, genetically and physically, a unique individual exists: "Once it is alive, it is totally there as this particular actual being, even though it is only partially there as a *develope*d actuality. *There is no such thing as a potentially living organism.*"[50]

The zygote is a person because it can evolve into nothing else; the essence of its personhood already exists:

> No individual living body can "become" a person unless it already is a person. *No living being can become anything other than what it already essentially is. . . . Only artifacts, such as clocks and spaceships, come into existence part by part. Living beings come into existence all at once and then gradually unfold to themselves and to the world what they already, but only incipiently, are.* Some developmentalists use the analogy of the blueprint in characterizing the zygote. But a blueprint never becomes part of a house, unless it is used to paper the walls.[51]

So what does all this mean? It means that in abortion we are killing living human beings—human persons—and that no one can afford not to be concerned about this issue.

5. *What really happens during an abortion?*

One of the major reasons that abortion is tolerated in this country is because people cannot see the procedures and the effects of those procedures upon the little child in the womb. Even our own television programs on abortion were censored. TV stations would not permit them to be shown. This is the very reason the film "The Silent Scream" (which showed an abortion in the womb) was so controversial and generated such emotion. It visually and viscerally demonstrated the results of abortion upon an 11-week-old girl:

> This film, using new sonographic techniques, shows the outline of the child in the womb thrashing to resist the suction device before it tears off the head. Then you see the dead child dismembered and the head crushed. Then the parts are sucked out.
>
> Nobody who sees this film will speak again of "painless" abortion. The doctor who performed the abortion couldn't bear to watch the film to the end. He rushed out of the room where it was shown and never performed another "procedure," though he had performed several thousand before.[52]

Those who *know* what happens in an abortion find it very difficult to condone the practice. The method used depends on the age of the pre-born, although more than one method may be necessary.

When an abortion occurs in the first 12 weeks, as most do, the baby is still small enough to be vacuumed out of the womb by a powerful suction machine—one with almost 25 times the force of a household vacuum cleaner.[53] In this method, known as suction curettage, the force of the vacuum literally tears or wrenches the child apart, limb by limb, until all that remains is the tiny little head. In any abortion the infant's head is too large to come through the suction tube itself, so the abortionist inserts forceps into the uterus. He uses these to grab the free-floating head, which he then crushes to a small enough size to fit into a suction tube. Then it, too, is removed.[54]

Dr. Nathanson describes this process, noting, "The baby is simply chopped up and pulled through the suction machine and emerges as just a pile of chopped meat."[55]

> As the suction tube is rotated within the womb, the membrane and fluid surrounding the fetus are quickly sucked away and the little being himself is soon torn apart. Finally the placenta, which is well connected to the lining of the uterus, is pulled away. One manual of instruction describes this phase of the abortion: "At any point that material is felt to be flowing into the tube, motion is stopped until the flow stops. Then the slow up and down gradual rotation pattern is continued. Blood-tinged fluid and bits of pink tissue will be seen flowing through the plastic tubing during the entire suction curettage."[56]

Another abortion procedure is called the D and E or "dilation and evacuation." The procedure is usually performed between the fourth and eighth months. The cervix is again dilated but, instead of suction, the forceps (resembling pliers) are inserted and clamped onto body parts, twisting them off and removing them in pieces. Then the spine and skull are crushed and extracted. The curettee or sharp, oval–shaped knife is then used to scrape out the uterus.

When D and C (dilation and curettage) is used, the knife is repeatedly put inside the womb and rotated. When resistance is encountered, the scraping is concentrated. In other words, a child may have its arms cut off, legs cut off, its face slashed and head cut off, and its body mutilated and cut into small pieces. The body parts and placenta are then suctioned out.[57] The technical term for methodologically cutting the baby to pieces is "morcellation." These procedures are potentially dangerous.

Any time an abortion is performed which cuts or sucks the child to pieces, the body parts must be carefully reassembled to verify a "complete" infant now exists outside the womb. The reason for this is the danger from infection should any body part of the child be left in the womb. A paper presented to the Association of Planned Parenthood physicians in 1978 described the D and E technique in this manner: "The fetus was extracted in small pieces to minimize cervical trauma. The fetal head was often the most difficult object to crush and remove because of its size and contour. The operator kept track of each portion of the fetal skeleton. . . ."[58]

The "saline method"—salt poisoning—is another abortion procedure that is used between four and seven months. This was the most common method employed throughout the 1970s.[59] In this procedure, a 3 1/2-to 4-inch needle is inserted through the stomach wall of the mother into the amniotic sac. Two hundred milliliters of amniotic fluid are withdrawn and replaced with a powerful salt solution. In this procedure the child swallows salt, as well as "breathes" it in. In essence, the child is slowly poisoned while the salt is burning the skin over the entire body. The mother goes into labor and expels a dead, badly burned, and shriveled baby. Occasionally, babies who survive the procedure are born with severe complications because, "Through this process the tissues and organs of the child begin to hemorrhage and are destroyed. Huge bruises appear all over the body surfaces as arteries and veins rupture."[60]

Other abortions are induced using the chemical prostaglandin. The prostaglandin consists of hormone-like compounds which are injected or applied to the uterine muscle, causing fetal circulatory damage, intense contractions, and the expelling of the baby. Because prostaglandin is not directly lethal to the pre-born, such abortions result in far more live births than with the saline method. These unexpected live births are extremely difficult on medical staff and particularly the mother: "Gasping for air, twitching and moving about, babies born struggling to survive abortion are unforgettable to their mothers. After watching these infants die, the scene is replayed mentally over and over again, and a cycle of self punishment may begin."[61]

Usually, when the child is born alive, it is simply permitted to starve to death. But there are cases where it has been strangled or killed.

In fact, these abortions are so difficult to bear that the "dilation and evacuation" method was developed specifically to avoid the problems of live birth. By cutting, crushing, or poisoning the child to death while still "hidden" in the womb, the results were still lethal but "less visible" to the mother and medical staff. Regardless, the consequences to medical staff remains. For example:

> In Hawaii, McDermott and Char reported that "the nurses themselves felt that they had replaced the illicit underground abortionists in other cities, and, like them, they were personally involved in the slicing and chopping up of 'babies' (the word they used to describe expelled fetal parts and fetuses that were warm and sometimes breathing)." . . .
>
> Physicians are no more immune. Many countries have reported increased depressive reactions and breakdowns among their guilt-ridden doctors.[62, cf. 63]

One more method is called the hysterotomy (six to eight months). The only difference between this method and a Caesarean section is that the whole point of the operation is to kill the child, not to save it. An incision is made through the abdomen into the womb, the baby is removed and allowed to die by neglect—or killed by strangulation while still inside the mother (the baby cannot be strangled outside the womb). It's ironic that once the child is outside the womb it cannot be killed; otherwise, the physician is legally guilty of murder. Legally, it can only be left to die by starvation.[64]

6. Does the baby feel pain during an abortion?

As early as 1981, it was strongly suspected by some researchers that pre-born children were capable of feeling pain as soon as eight weeks or 56 days.[65] (Today this figure may be even lower.)

Dr. Nathanson states, "I think the baby probably feels pain in all of them [abortion procedures,] [although] the degree, the sophistication of the [pain] perception certainly varies with the length of gestation . . . [but]

there's really little question that pain is felt in some degree or other during an abortion."[66] Whatever the sensation of pain, there is little doubt that the vast majority of abortions cause pain to the child.

John T. Noonan, Jr., professor in the School of Law at University of California, Berkeley, describes how these abortion procedures are painful to the pre-born:

> Are these experiences painful? The application of a sharp knife to the skin and the destruction of vital tissue cannot but be a painful experience for any sentient creature. It lasts for about ten minutes.
>
> Being subjected to a vacuum is painful, as is dismemberment by suction. The time from the creation of the vacuum to the chief destruction of the child again is about ten minutes.
>
> Hypertonic saline solution causes what is described as "exquisite and severe pain" if, by accident during an abortion, it enters subcutaneously the body of the woman having the abortion. It is inferable that the unborn would have an analogous experience lasting some two hours, as the saline solution takes about this long to work before the fetal heart stops.
>
> The impact of prostaglandins constricting the circulation of the blood or impairing the heart must be analogous to that when these phenomena occur in born children: they are not pleasant. . . .
>
> An observation of Melzack is of particular pertinence: the local injection of hypertonic saline opens the spinal gate, he has remarked, and evokes severe pain. . . . The general observation of Melzack on the mechanism of pain is also worth recalling: any lesion which impairs the tonic inhibitory influence from the brain opens the gate, with a consequent increase of pain. Any method of abortion which results first in damage to the cortex may have the initial effect of increasing the pain sensations.[67]

Noonan makes another important point. As cruel as

such pain is, it is not the real issue. The real issue is the death of the child in the first place:

> Whatever the method used, the unborn are experiencing the greatest of bodily evils, the ending of their lives. They are undergoing the death agony. However inarticulate, however slight their cognitive powers, however rudimentary their sensations, they are sentient creatures undergoing the disintegration of their being and the termination of their vital capabilities. That experience is painful in itself.[68]

It is truly incredible that in an age where great amounts of money and effort are expended saving whales, baby seals, trees, bald eagles, three-inch fish, and even *weeds*—in an era of great concern over "animal and environmental rights"—not only do we deny the rights of the unborn to life, we callously turn our heads to their suffering. We not only treat them as less than human, we treat them as having less value than animals and weeds. Dogs, for example, have far more rights in this country than unborn children.

This is one reason why a group of physicians, including two past presidents of the American College of Obstetricians and Gynecologists (Dr. Richard Schmidt and Dr. Fred Hofmeister) wrote to President Reagan in support of disseminating the truth that the fetus does experience pain. They stated, "Over the last 18 years, real time ultrasonography, fetoscopy, study of the fetal EKG . . . and fetal EEG (electroencephalogram) have demonstrated the remarkable responsiveness of the human fetus to pain, touch, and sound."[69]

7. *What do some women feel during an abortion?*

Millions of women have now learned firsthand what the abortion technique does to their pre-born infant. Some women with later abortions (second or third trimester) tell horror stories of feeling their babies thrashing around, attempting to escape the consequences of the saline poison, the chemicals, or even the forceps and knife.

Physicians know full well what happens to the unborn

baby. For example, one doctor who performs saline abortions describes it this way:

> All of a sudden one notices that at the time of the saline infusion there is a lot of activity in the uterus. That's not fluid currents. That's obviously the fetus being distressed by swallowing the concentrated salt solution and kicking violently—[that's part of] the death drama.[70]

If physicians are bothered by observing these experiences, what do you think the mothers feel when experiencing the child dying within them?

Nancy Jo Mann is the founder of "Women Exploited By Abortion" (WEBA). After seeking an abortion earlier in her life, she realized that she had been deliberately lied to by her abortionist counselors. She was also never informed of the risks. She describes her experience in these heart-wrenching words:

> After the fluid was withdrawn, he injected 200 cc's of the saline solution—half a pint of concentrated salt solution. From then on, it was terrible.
>
> My baby began thrashing about—it was like a boxing match. She was in pain. The saline was burning her skin, her eyes, her throat. It was choking her, making her sick. She was in agony, trying to escape. . . .
>
> For some reason it had never entered my mind that with an abortion she would have to die. I had never wanted my baby to die; I only wanted to get rid of my "problem."
>
> But it was too late to turn back now. There was no way to save her.
>
> So instead I talked to her. I tried to comfort her. I tried to ease her pain. I told her I didn't want to do this to her, but it was too late to stop it. I didn't want her to die. I begged her not to die. I told her I was sorry, to forgive me, that I was wrong, that I didn't want to kill her. For two hours I could feel her struggling inside me.

But then, as suddenly as it began, she stopped. Even today, I remember her very last kick on my left side. She had no strength left. She gave up and died.

Despite my grief and guilt, I was relieved that her pain was finally over. But I was never the same again. The abortion killed not only my daughter; it killed a part of me.

Before that needle had entered my abdomen, I had liked myself. . . . When the child I had abandoned suddenly began its struggle within me, I hated myself. It was that fast. Every bit of self-esteem, every value I held dear, every hope of which I had ever dreamed—all were stripped away by the poison of that one vain act. Every memory of joy was now tainted by the stench of death. . . .

There was no way to stop it. There was no way to put everything back the way it had been. I no longer had any control, any choice. I was powerless. I was weak. I was a murderer.

A little while after my baby stopped moving they gave me an intravenous injection to help stimulate labor. I was in hard labor for 12 hours, all through the night. When finally I delivered, the nurses didn't make it into my room in time.

I delivered my daughter myself at 5:30 the next morning, October 31. After I delivered her, I held her in my hands. I looked her over from top to bottom. She had a head of hair, and her eyes were opening. I looked at her little tiny feet and hands. Her fingers and toes even had little fingernails and swirls of fingerprints. Everything was perfect. She was not a "fetus." She was not a "product of conception." She was a tiny human being. . . . She was my daughter. Twisted with agony, silent and still. Dead.

It seemed like I held her for 10 minutes or more, but it was probably only 30 seconds—because as soon as the nurses came rushing in, they grabbed her from my hands and threw her—literally threw her—into a bed pan and carried her away.

To add insult to injury, after my daughter was taken away, they brought another woman into the room to finish the last hour of her labor. But this woman wasn't having an abortion. No, she had a beautiful, healthy baby boy. No words can describe how rough that was on me.

I was released from the hospital 8 hours after the delivery. The official report filled out by my abortionist stated that the procedure had been completed with "no complications.". . . Soon afterwards I began to withdraw from those who loved me, especially from my family since they had supported and encouraged me to have the abortion. . . .

Three weeks after my abortion, I chose to be sterilized by tubal ligation. I couldn't cope with the idea that I could ever possibly kill again. It was too devastating. . . .

I became preoccupied with thoughts of death. I fantasized about how I would die. My baby had struggled for two hours. I've tried to imagine myself dying a similar kind of death. . . .

Four months after my abortion, the bleeding and infection were still persistent. Too ashamed to go to my own Ob/Gyn, I returned to Dr. Fong and he performed a D and C to clean out the uterus. He cut off my cervix and left the packing inside of me. Three weeks later I was grossly rotted out inside.

Seven months later, at 22 years of age, I was forced to undergo a total hysterectomy—all because of that "safe and easy," legal abortion. By this time, I didn't care if I lived or died anymore. . . . I hated the world only as much as I hated myself."[71]

What can "pro-choice" people possibly say to something like this?

8. Is abortion a perfectly safe procedure for women? What are the physical risks?

Most people continue to believe that abortion is a safe procedure—at least for the mother. Those who support abortion in this country constantly inform us that there is nothing to be concerned about.

But this view is incorrect. After examining "the vast body of the world's medical literature on the subject,"

Thomas W. Hilgers, M.D., concluded, "The medical hazards of legally induced abortion are very significant and should be conscientiously weighed."[72]

Hundreds of thousands of women have already paid a physical price and many have paid the ultimate physical price for their abortion: Thousands have died.[73]

Here is a brief list of the possible physical consequences that can come to those having abortions:

> Death
> Perforation of the uterus
> Bleeding requiring transfusion (with possible hepatitis or AIDS infection)
> Tearing of the cervix, with unknown impact upon cervical competence during subsequent pregnancies
> Anesthesia-related accidents, including convulsions, shock, and cardiac arrest from toxic reaction to the anesthetic used
> Pelvic inflammatory disease and possible associated infertility
> Unintended surgery, including laparotomy, hysterotomy, and hysterectomy
> Bladder perforation
> Bowel perforation
> Persistent bleeding
> Tissue retention
> Anemia
> Peritonitis (a serious infection of the membranous coat lining the abdominal cavity)
> Minor infections and fever of unknown origin
> Undetected tubal pregnancy
> Pulmonary emboli (obstruction of the pulmonary artery)
> Venous thrombophlebitis (inflammation of a vein developing before a blood clot)
> Depression
> Psychosis
> Suicide[74]

Many women who have experienced such problems are now angry over never being warned of such consequences prior to the abortion. The unfortunate fact is that none of these consequences can be predicted in advance. The woman who has an abortion is playing Russian roulette not only with the health of her body but also with her ability to conceive in the future, with her own mental health, and even with the health of future children.[75]

Here are some official health statistics that reveal the dangers attached to having an abortion. Consider the following data:

> Studies show that 20 to 30% of all suction and D and C abortions performed in hospitals will result in long term, negative side effects relating primarily to fertility and reproduction.[76]

> First, every type of abortion procedure carries significant risks. . . . Overall, the rate of immediate and short term complications is no less than 10 percent. . . . The evidence indicates that the actual morbidity rate is probably much higher.[77]

> The technique of saline abortion was originally developed in the concentration camps of Nazi Germany. In Japan, where abortion has been legalized since the 1940's, the saline abortion technique has been outlawed because it is "extremely dangerous." Indeed, in the United States saline abortion is second only to heart transplants as the elective surgery with the highest fatality rate. Despite this fact, state laws attempting to prohibit saline abortions because of their great risks to aborting women have been declared unconstitutional by the courts.[78]

> Frequent complications associated with prostaglandin abortions include spontaneous ruptures in the uterine wall, convulsions, hemorrhage, coagulation defects, and cervical injury. Incomplete abortions are also very common.[79]

> A high risk of infection is common to all forms of abortion.[80]

> Studies have shown that a woman's risk of

an ectopic pregnancy dramatically increases following an abortion. . . . Treatment of an ectopic pregnancy requires major surgery. . . . [In addition,] according to one study, the risk of a second trimester miscarriage increases tenfold following a vaginal abortion.[81]

Even the abortion-induced death rates are in all probability underreported and should be of much greater concern.

What should be clear is that there is a major flaw in the mortality statistics for legal abortion. It is quite possible that only 5 to 10 percent of all deaths resulting from legal abortion are being reported as abortion-related. Even if 50 percent were being accurately reported, that extra margin of risk is far greater than women are being led to believe. Indeed, based on the *reported* abortion deaths alone, abortion is already the fifth leading cause of maternal death in the United States.

The most common causes of death from legal abortion include: hemorrhage, infection, blood clots in the lungs, heart failure, and anesthetic complications. These can occur after any type of abortion procedure and are generally unpredictable. . . . More frequently the death occurs *after* the patient leaves the clinic. . . .

Furthermore, it should be noted that abortion actually increases the chance of maternal death in later pregnancies.[82]

It is obvious that the abortion industry has everything to gain and nothing to lose by withholding data concerning the physical consequences of abortion.

9. Are there also psychological consequences to abortion?

The Royal College of Obstetricians and Gynecologists, in a survey of available psychiatric and psychological studies, found that there were serious psychological problems that developed in many women after their abortions. The Royal College reported, "The incidence of serious, permanent psychiatric aftermath is variously reported as between 9 and 59 percent."[83]

Even Washington psychiatrist-obstetrician Julius Fogel, a doctor who performs abortions, admitted in 1971 before the Supreme Court decision, "I think every woman . . . has a trauma at destroying a pregnancy . . . she is destroying herself . . . a psychological price is paid. . . . Something happens on the deepest levels of a woman's consciousness when she destroys a pregnancy. I know that as a psychiatrist."[84]

In a 1989 interview he noted (by this time he had performed some 20,000 abortions), "There is no question about the emotional grief and mourning following an abortion. . . . Many come in [to the office even years later] —some are just mute, some hostile. Some burst out crying. . . . There is no question in my mind we are disturbing a life process."[85]

This whole phenomenon of psychological aftereffects which take place following abortions is known as the "post abortion syndrome.[86] Early studies have assumed that this syndrome would appear within a few months after the abortion, but it appears that with the majority of women it can be 5 to even 35 years later. Since abortion has only been legalized in this country since 1973, of course no one can "scientifically, statistically" prove harmful long-term effects. But the data currently being gathered are more and more pointing to the devastating effects of post-abortion syndrome:

> A European study reported negative psychiatric manifestations following legal abortions in 55 percent of the women examined by psychiatrists.
>
> In the *American Journal of Psychiatry*, researchers reported that of 500 aborted

women studied, 43 percent showed immediate negative responses. At the time of a later review . . . up to 10 percent of the women were classified as having developed "serious psychiatric complications."

In one of the most detailed studies of post-abortion sequelae: "Anxiety, which if present after an abortion is felt very keenly, was reported by 43.1 percent . . . . Depression, one of the emotions likely to be felt with more than a moderate strength, was reported by 31.9 percent of women surveyed . . . 26.4 percent felt guilt . . . [and] 18.1 percent felt no relief or just a bit. They were overwhelmed by negative feelings. Even those women who were strongly supportive of the right to abort reacted to their own abortions with regret, anger, embarrassment, fear of disapproval and even shame."

In another paper, the same group of psychiatrists reported that when detailed interviews were performed, every aborted woman, "without exception" experienced "feelings of guilt or profound regret. . . . All the women felt that they had lost an important part of themselves.". . .

One doctor reports: "Since abortion was legalized I have seen hundreds of patients who have had the operation. Approximately 10% expressed very little or no concern. . . . Among the other 90 percent there were all shades of distress, anxiety, heartache and remorse."[87]

Abortion cannot help but produce feelings of guilt and depression in most women. But in some women this also increases the risk of suicide. Studies concerning abortion and suicide reveal:

Feelings of rejection, low self-esteem, guilt and depression are all ingredients for suicide, and the rate of suicide attempts among aborted women is phenomenally high. According to one study, women who have had abortions are nine times more likely to attempt suicide than women in the general population.

The fact of high suicide rates among aborted women is well known among professionals who counsel suicidal persons. . . . There has been a dramatic rise in the suicide rate since the early 1970s when abortion was first legalized. Between 1978 and 1981 alone, the suicide rate among teenagers increased 500 percent.[88]

Abortion has also been identified as the cause of psychotic and schizophrenic reactions. Symptoms frequently include extreme anxiety and feelings of paranoia.[89]

Although most abortion peddlers promise us that it is the *women* they are most concerned about, it is the women they may also help to destroy.

Anyone who has examined only a few dozen of the 300+ studies conducted on the psychological aftermath of abortion cannot doubt that abortions cause psychological problems to women.[90] What is difficult to believe is the irresponsibility of those who claim it has been "proven" that there are no psychological dangers.

If so, why are there now tens of thousands of women in groups such as American Victims of Abortion (AVA), Victims of Choice, Women Exploited By Abortion (WEBA), Post Abortion Counseling and Education (PACE), Healing Visions Network, and others? Why do hundreds of health-care workers attend annual conferences at the University of Notre Dame on post-abortion counseling when there is no need?[91]

On March 16, 1989, Congress itself heard testimony of the psychological dangers of abortion from psychologist Wanda Franz, Ph.D., in a special hearing on the medical and psychological impact of abortion:[92]

Women who report negative after-effects from abortion know exactly what their problem is. . . . They report horrible nightmares of children calling to them from trash cans, of body parts, and blood. When they are reminded of the abortion," she continued, "the women re-experienced it with terrible psychological pain. . . . They feel worthless and victimized because they failed at the most natural of human activities—the role of being a mother."[93]

Other studies, such as the *Report on the Psychological Aftermath of Abortion*[94] concluded:*

The list of psychological abreactions [later responses] to induced abortion is lengthy [in the research literature] and worthy of explication [explanation]: guilt, depression, grief, anxiety, sadness, shame, helplessness and hopelessness, lowered self-esteem, distrust, hostility toward self and others, regret, sleep disorders, recurring dreams, nightmares, anniversary reactions, psychophysiological symptoms, suicidal ideation and behavior, alcohol and/or chemical dependencies, sexual dysfunction, insecurity, numbness, painful re-experiencing of the abortion, relationship disruption, communication impairment and/or restriction, isolation, fetal fantasies, self-condemnation, flashbacks, uncontrollable weeping, eating disorders, preoccupation, confused and/or distorted thinking, bitterness, and a sense of loss and emptiness.[96]

Further, this report cited several of the same problems found in other reports concerning the reluctance of women to report serious problems.[97]

Finally, the report concluded that the studies with the most flaws are those most likely to report positive outcomes.[98] Also, it is likely that even the data currently available "under-represent the extent of the negative psychological aftermath of post abortion."[99]

---

*Discovery, verification, and large-scale epidemiological assessment are usually the three phases of research progression. This report noted that in the case of post-abortion reactions, only the first phase of research had been conducted, with the observation that the need for phase two has been demonstrated and the recommendation that it proceed.[95]

In conclusion, the promoters of abortion may claim that abortion is always safe, but this is a lie. (There is also good evidence that abortion even affects the siblings of the pre-born child.[100])

10. What does the Bible teach about abortion?

In the Old Testament, the Bible uses the same Hebrew words to describe the pre-born child, infants, and children. In the New Testament, the same Greek words also describe the pre-born child, infants and children which indicates a continuity from conception to childhood and on into adulthood.

The Greek word *brephos* is often used of the newly-born, infants, and older children (Luke 2:12,16; 18:15; 1 Peter 2:2). For example, in Acts 7:19 *brephos* refers to the children killed at Pharaoh's command. But in Luke 1:41,44 this same word is used of John the Baptist while he was yet in the womb, a pre-born infant.

In God's eyes he was indistinguishable from a child. The biblical writer also informs us that John was filled with the Holy Spirit while still in his mother's womb, indicating personhood (Luke 1:15). Even three months before birth, John could miraculously recognize Jesus in Mary's womb (Luke 1:44).

In addition, the Greek *huios* means "son" but is used in Luke 1:36 of John the Baptist's existence in the womb before birth (at six months).

The Hebrew word *yeled* is usually used of children (i.e., a child, boy, etc.). But in Exodus 21:22 it is used of a child in the womb. In Genesis 25:22 the word *yeladim* (children) is used of Rebecca's children struggling while in her womb. In Job 3:3, Job uses the word *geber* to describe his conception: "A man child is conceived." But *geber* is a Hebrew noun that is usually translated as "man," "male," or "husband." In Job 3:11-16, Job equates the pre-born child with kings, counselors, and princes.

All these Scriptures and many others indicate that God does not make a distinction between potential life and real life, or in delineating stages of personhood—namely, between a pre-born infant in the womb at any stage and a born infant or child. The Scripture repeatedly assumes the continuity of a person from conception to adulthood.

In fact, no separate word is used exclusively of the pre-born that will permit it to be distinguished from an infant as far as its personhood and value are concerned.

Further, God Himself relates to the unborn as persons. In Psalm 139:16 the Psalmist says concerning God, "Your eyes saw my unformed body." The writer used the word *golem*, translated as "body" or "substance," to describe himself while he was in the womb. He uses this term to refer to God's personal care for him even during the first part of the embryonic state (from implantation up to the first few weeks), the state *before* the fetus is physically "formed" into a miniature human being. We know that the embryo is "unformed" for only four or five weeks. In other words, even in the "unformed body" stage of gestation (0-4 weeks), God says that He is caring for and molding a child (Psalm 139:13-16).

Other Scriptures also indicate that God relates to the fetus as a person. Job 31:15 says, "Did not he who *made me in the womb* make them? Did not the same one form us both within our mothers?"

In Job 10:8,12 we read, "Your hands *shaped me and made me.* [You] clothed me with skin and flesh and knit me together with bones and sinews."

Psalm 78:5,6 reveals God's concern over "the children yet to be born."

Psalm 139:13-16 states, "For you *created my inmost being*; you *knit me together* in my mother's womb. I praise you because I am fearfully and wonderfully made. . . . My frame was not hidden from you when I was made in the secret place. When I was woven together in the depths of the earth, your eyes saw my unformed body."

These Scriptures reveal that personal pronouns are used to describe the relationship between God and those in the womb.

These verses and others (Jeremiah 1:5; Galatians 1:15,16; Isaiah 49:1,5) show that God views the pre-born children in the womb as persons. No other conclusion is possible. We must agree with theologian John Frame, "There is nothing in Scripture that even remotely suggests that the unborn child is anything less than a human person from the moment of conception."[101]

In light of the above we must concede that those

Scriptures which indicate human life belongs to God, not to us, prohibit abortion. The Bible teaches that people ultimately belong to God because all men are created by Him.

The Scriptures teach that men are "the offspring of God" (Acts 17:29 NASB) and that "in Him we live and move and exist" (Acts 17:28 NASB). Malachi could ask, "Have we not all one Father? Did not one God create us?" (Malachi 2:10).

The Scriptures teach that God "Himself gives to all life and breath and all things" (Acts 17:25 NASB) because He "made the world and all things in it" (Acts 17:24 NASB). Understanding this, Isaiah could say "O LORD, Thou art our Father, we are the clay, and Thou our potter; and all of us are the work of Thy hand" (Isaiah 64:8).

The psalmist could also say, "The earth is the LORD'S, and everything in it, the world, and all who live in it" (Psalm 24:1).

Further, the Scriptures teach, "Your hands made me and formed me" (Psalm 119:73) and "The LORD . . . forms the spirit of man within him" (Zechariah 12:1 NASB).

God Himself makes the statement, "Behold, all souls are Mine; the soul of the father as well as the soul of the son is Mine" (Ezekiel 18:4 NASB).

Since all life was created by God and belongs to Him, no one has the right to kill something God has created (Exodus 20:13).

Scriptures also teach we must defend and protect the weak, the defenseless, the innocent, the needy. This surely includes unborn children. Consider the following Scriptures which indicate God's concern for those who cannot speak on their own behalf.

> Proverbs 31:8,9—Speak up for those who cannot speak for themselves, for the rights of all who are destitute. Speak up and judge fairly; defend the rights of the poor and needy.
>
> Psalm 82:2-4—How long will you defend the unjust and show partiality to the wicked? Defend the cause of the weak and fatherless; maintain the rights of the poor and oppressed. Rescue the weak and needy; deliver them from the hand of the wicked.

The Bible has many Scriptures like this. There can be no doubt that they also apply to the innocent unborn who are the *most* defenseless, innocent, and needy. Indeed, God will hold us accountable for their welfare:

"Rescue those being led away to death; hold back those staggering toward slaughter. If you say, 'But we knew nothing about this,' does not he who weighs the heart perceive it? Does not he who guards your life know it? Will he not repay each person according to what he has done?" (Proverbs 24:11,12)

In fact, numerous Scriptures condemn the killing of innocent life (Proverbs 6:16-19; 12:6; Deuteronomy 19:10; 27:25). Many of the following Scriptures apply to those who perform abortions.

> Isaiah 1:15—When you spread out your hands in prayer, I will hide my eyes from you; even if you offer many prayers, I will not listen. Your hands are full of blood.
>
> Isaiah 59:2,3,4b,7b—But your iniquities have separated you from your God; your sins have hidden his face from you, so that he will not hear. For your hands are stained with blood, your fingers with guilt. Your lips have spoken lies, and your tongue mutters wicked things. . . . They rely on empty arguments and speak lies; they conceive trouble and give birth to evil. . . . Their thoughts are evil thoughts; ruin and destruction mark their ways.
>
> Jeremiah 22:17 (NASB)—But your eyes and your heart are intent only upon your own dishonest gain, and on shedding innocent blood and on practicing oppression and extortion.
>
> Hebrews 4:13—Nothing in all creation is hidden from God's sight. Everything is uncovered and laid bare before the eyes of him to whom we must give account.

Can one imagine Jesus accepting the idea of abortion? Did He not teach: "See that you do not despise one of these little ones, for I say to you, that their angels in heaven continually behold the face of My Father who is in heaven. . . . Thus it is not the will of your Father who is in heaven that one of these little ones perish" (Matthew 18:10,14 NASB).

Another way to decide whether abortion is a justifiable practice is to think through the implications of the Incarnation of Jesus Christ. The question is, At what point was the personhood of Jesus present?

In brief, it *had* to be present at the point of conception. Both the New Testament and the doctrinal creeds of the church affirm that God became man at the point of conception. The eternal Son of God became incarnate in Mary's womb. Christ's personal history on earth began not when He was "born of the virgin" but when He was "conceived by the Holy Spirit" (Luke 1:31,35).

It is significant that God chose to begin the process of incarnation at the point of conception rather than at some other point. But Christ "had to be made like His brethren in all things" (Hebrews 2:17 NASB); His human history, like ours, had to begin at conception.

Lawyers Herbert T. Krimmel and Martin J. Foley argue that because Jesus was fully present at conception so must every other person be as well:

> Now, given the facts established by Holy Scripture that (a) Christ was fully God and fully man and (b) Christ was conceived by the Holy Ghost, our argument can be stated succinctly:
>
> 1. "Conception" literally means the process which terminates the initial presence in the womb of that which is conceived (i.e., the single cell entity referred to in biological terms as a zygote). Consequently, when one says that Mary conceived by the activity of the Holy Ghost, one must mean that which the Holy Ghost produced in and through conception was the initial presence of the zygote.
>
> 2. The zygote the Holy Ghost brought about in Mary's womb was Jesus Christ, true God and true man, in His human nature like man in all things except for sin.
>
> 3. If Jesus (true God and true man) was

present in His mother's womb from the first moment of His conception, then it follows that other men must also be alive and existing as human beings from the first moments of their conceptions; for unless they are the same as Jesus in this respect of their human nature, He would not be like them in every essential human respect except for sin. This is to say, then, that a human being must be fully present as such from the moment of conception.[102]

Finally, the Bible teaches that the fetus in the womb at *any* stage is valued as highly as any adult life. Where does the Bible teach this? Exodus 21:22-25 states,

If men who are fighting hit a pregnant woman and she gives birth prematurely but there is no serious injury, the offender must be fined whatever the woman's husband demands and the court allows. But if there is serious injury, you are to take life for life, eye for eye, tooth for tooth, hand for hand, foot for foot, burn for burn, wound for wound, bruise for bruise.

Distinguished Jewish exegete Umberto Cassuto interprets and translates Exodus 21:22-25 in his celebrated *Commentary on the Book of Exodus:*

When men strive together and they hurt unintentionally a woman with child, and her children come forth but no mischief happens —that is, the woman and the children do not die—the one who hurt her shall surely be punished by a fine. But if any mischief happened, that is, if the woman dies or the children die, then you shall give life for life.[103]

Keil and Delitzsch in their Old Testament commentary on the book of Exodus explain that the passage demands exactly the same penalty for injuring the mother as the child.[104] There is absolutely no ground to differentiate between the mother or the child in this context if we keep to the rights of language.

Distinguished Hebrew scholar Dr. Gleason Archer has stated about this passage:

> There is no ambiguity here whatever. What is required is that if there should be an injury either to the mother or to her children, the injury shall be avenged by a like injury to the assailant. If it involves the life, the *nephesh*, of the premature baby, then the assailant shall pay for it with his life. There is no second class status attached to the fetus under this rule. The fetus is just as valuable as the mother. It is as if he were a normally delivered child or an older person. The penalty is life for life.[105]

The sixth commandment, "Thou shalt not kill" (the Hebrew is "murder") refers to every act of murder: child, wife, husband, stranger, self, etc. Since it is scientifically established that the fetus *is* a human being, the commandment applies to abortion as well. "Thou shalt not kill" is equivalent to "Thou shalt not commit abortion."

All of the above and a great deal more Scriptures indicate that the Bible is not silent on abortion. To the contrary, a biblical understanding of God, man, procreation and conception, gestation, and life itself reveals that far from being silent on abortion, the Bible implies that abortion is a crime against both God and man.

11. What about the viability of the "pro-choice" arguments?

In our *When Does Life Begin? And 39 Other Tough Questions About Abortion*, we spent 100 pages examining all the specific pro-choice arguments given by proponents of abortion. Among them we included, "Why doesn't life begin at viability?" "Is abortion really murder?" "How does abortion affect siblings?" "What are the theological implications of abortion?" "What really happened in the Supreme Court's Roe v. Wade decision?" "Shouldn't abortion be allowed so that only 'wanted babies' will be brought into the world?" "Isn't it true that human life is routinely destroyed in miscarriage and in vitro fertilization?" "Aren't there certain hard cases where abortion is clearly justified such as rape, threat to the life of the mother, incest, and the possibility of deformity?" "Don't opinion polls favor abortion?" "Won't recriminalization of abortion increase illegal abortions and force women into dangerous 'back alley' operations?" "Aren't there too many people in the world already?" "If abortion is criminalized, won't women go to jail?" "Aren't pro-life people trying to punish women?" "What about abortion and birth control pills?" "Won't the criminalization of abortion cause the poor to suffer while the rich will simply continue to get abortions?" "Who is going to decide that an abortion may or may not occur—the individual or the state?" and "Isn't it true that pro-abortion is forced abortion where pro-choice is only for the right to choose?"

After examining all of these arguments and others, we found ourselves forced to conclude with professor of philosophy James M. Humber who wrote in *Bio-Medical Ethics and the Law* that "none of the major defenses of abortion succeeds in its purpose" and "the arguments of the pro-abortionists are all so poor that they should not be accepted at face value, but rather should be seen as after-the-fact rationalizations for belief held to be true on other grounds."[106] We would refer interested readers to our book for further analysis of the "pro-choice" position.

Conclusion: What if you have had an abortion?

Have you had an abortion? Wherever you are, we want you to know that genuine forgiveness and inner peace are possible, that real freedom from the past can be experienced.

God is a forgiving God:

> But you are a forgiving God, gracious and compassionate, slow to anger and abounding in love (Nehemiah 9:17b).
> You are forgiving and good, O Lord, abounding in love to all who call to you (Psalm 86:5).

In fact, God not only forgives, He actually "forgets":

> I, even I, am he who blots out your transgressions, for my own sake, and remembers your sins no more (Isaiah 43:25).

You can find forgiveness right now simply by trusting in Jesus Christ. You can trust in Christ by turning from your own ways, acknowledging and confessing your sins, and turning to Christ with the confidence that through His power He will give you forgiveness and new life. If you desire to have your sins forgiven, to be free of all guilt, to have new life in Christ, to know God, and to know you are loved by Him, the following prayer is suggested:

> Dear God, I do confess my sin. My abortion was wrong and I now come to You asking for Your forgiveness and cleansing. I ask that You will not only forgive this sin, but will forgive all the sins of my life. I accept that Jesus Christ is God, that He died on the cross to pay the penalty for my sins, was resurrected on the third day, and is living today. I now receive Him as my Lord and Savior. I now accept the forgiveness that You so freely provided on the cross and promised me in the Bible. Make Your forgiveness real to me. I ask this in Jesus' name. Amen.

Becoming a Christian involves a serious commitment. Please attend a church where Christ is honored and write us here at The Ankerberg Theological Research Institute for helpful materials on living the Christian Life (P.O. Box 8977, Chattanooga, TN 37414).

Footnotes

1. John Warwick Montgomery, "The Rights of the Unborn Children," *The Simon Greenleaf Law Review*, vol. 5 (1985-86), p. 25.

2. Michael Tooley, *Abortion and Infanticide* (Oxford: Calendon Press, 1983), p. 419.

3. William Brennan, *Medical Holocausts: Exterminative Medicine in Nazi Germany and Contemporary America* (Boston, MA: Nordland Pub. International, Inc., 1980), vol. 1, p. 98.

4. Peter Singer, as cited by Martin Maywer in *Fundamentalist Journal*, June 1988.

5. Paul Fowler, *Abortion: Toward an Evangelical Consensus* (Portland, OR: Multnomah Press, 1987), p. 11; "Abortion: Hard Questions and Elusive Answers," *USA Today*, April 24, 1984; Americans United for Life Legal Defense Fund, "On Pain Experienced by Fetuses in Abortions" (Chicago, IL: AUFLDF, compiled data, nd.), cf. *Chicago Sun Times*, "26 Doctors Agree: Fetuses Feel Pain," Feb. 14, 1984.

6. Lawyer Cooperative, *U.S. Supreme Court Reports*, vol. 35 (1974), *Roe v. Wade*, 410 US 113, p. 181; 410 US 113 at 159; cf. Harold O. J. Brown, *Death Before Birth* (Nashville, TN: Thomas Nelson, 1977), p. 81, cf. pp. 73-96; John Warwick Montgomery, "The Rights of the Unborn Children," *The Simon Greenleaf Law Review*, vol. 5 (1985-86), p. 64.

7. Motion filed in the Supreme Court of the United States, Oct. 15, 1971 (Re: No. 70-18 and No. 70-40), titled *Motion and Brief Amicus Curiae of Certain Physicians, Professionals and Fellows of the American College of Obstetrics and Gynecology in Support of Appellees*, Dennis J. Horan et al., United States District Court 1971, pp. 19, 29-30.

8. Ibid., p. 7.

9. Ibid., pp. 13-14.

10. Ibid., p. 64, cf. pp. 19-20, 58-64.

11. Television program transcript, "Abortion," Chattanooga, TN, The John Ankerberg Evangelistic Association, 1982, p. 2.

12. *California Medicine*, vol. 113, no. 3 (Sept. 1970), p. 67.

13. Keith L. Moore, *The Developing Human: Clinically Oriented Embryology* (Philadelphia, PA: W.B. Sanders, 1982), p. 1, emphasis added.

14. Thomas W. Hilgers, Dennis J. Horan, *Abortion and Social Justice* (Thaxton, VA: Sun Life, 1980), p. 5.

15. *Encyclopedia and Dictionary of Medicine, Nursing and Allied Health* (Philadelphia: W.B. Sanders Co., 1978), 2nd ed., p. 335.

16. The Subcommittee on Separation of Powers, *Report to Senate Judiciary Committee* S-158, 97th Congress, First Session, 1981.

17. Ibid., cf. Richard Exley, *Abortion: Pro-life by Conviction, Pro-choice by Default* (Tulsa, OK: Honor Books, 1989), p. 18; Norman L. Geisler, *Christian Ethics: Options and Issues* (Grand Rapids, MI: Baker, 1989), p. 149.

18. Landrum B. Shettles, *Rites of Life: The Scientific Evidence for Life Before Birth* (Grand Rapids, MI: Zondervan, 1983), p. 114.

19. Ibid.

20. Ibid.

21. Ibid.

22. The Subcommittee on Separation of Powers, *Report to Senate Judiciary Committee* S-158, 97th Congress, First Session, 1981; cf. Richard Exley, *Abortion: Pro-life by Conviction, Pro-choice by Default* (Tulsa, OK: Honor Books, 1989), p. 18.

23. Ibid.; cf. Norman L. Geisler, *Christian Ethics: Options and Issues* (Grand Rapids, MI: Baker), 1989, p. 149.

24. Ibid., *Report to Senate*.

44

25. Ibid., and Richard Exley, *Abortion: Pro-life by Conviction, Pro-choice by Default* (Tulsa, OK: Honor Books, 1989), p. 18.
26. Dr. and Mrs. J. C. Willke, *Handbook on Abortion* and *Abortion Questions and Answers* (Hayes Publishing Co., 1985), p. 40.
27. Shettles, *Rites of Life: The Scientific Evidence for Life Before Birth*, p. 113.
28. The Subcommittee on Separation of Powers, *Report to Senate* ; cf. Exley, *Abortion: Pro-life by Conviction, Pro-choice by Default*, p. 18; Geisler, *Christian Ethics: Options and Issues*, p. 149.
29. Landrum B. Shettles in *Abortion: Opposing Viewpoints* (New York: Greenhaven Press, 1986), p. 16, emphasis added.
30. Hilgers and Horan, p. 317.
31. Ibid.
32. Ibid.
33. John C. Fletcher, Mark I. Evans, "Maternal Bonding in Early Fetal Ultrasound Examinations," *New England Journal of Medicine*, February 17, 1983.
34. Bernard N. Nathanson, "Deeper into Abortion," *New England Journal of Medicine*, Nov. 28, 1974, p. 1189.
35. Initial transcript, The Ankerberg Theological Research Institute, *Is Abortion Justifiable?* televised program, Jan. 1990, p. 7.
36. Geisler, *Christian Ethics: Options and Issues*, p. 140.
37. Hilgers and Horan, pp. 27, 32-33.
38. Jean S. Garton, *Who Broke the Baby?* (Minneapolis, MN: Bethany, 1979), p. 41. (Order from Life Cycle Books, 2205 Danforth Avenue, Toronto, Ontario M4C 1K4.)
39. Ibid., cf. Landrum B. Shettles in *Abortion: Opposing Viewpoints*, p. 19.
40. Geisler, *Christian Ethics: Options and Issues*, p. 140.
41. Garton, pp. 21-26.
42. Shettles in *Abortion: Opposing Viewpoints*, p. 19.
43. Lawyer Cooperative, *U.S. Supreme Court Reports*, p. 183; 410 US 113 at 163.
44. Ibid., pp. 180, 182; 410 US 113 at 158, 162.
45. Exley, *Abortion: Pro-life by Conviction, Pro-choice by Default*, p. 30.
46. Fowler, *Abortion: Toward an Evangelical Consensus*, p. 52.
47. Scientists for Life, Inc. and Edward C. Freiling, p. 40, emphasis added.
48. Geisler, *Christian Ethics: Options and Issues*, pp. 146-47.
49. Ibid., p. 154.
50. Hilgers, Horan and Mall (eds.), pp. 349-50, emphasis added.
51. Ibid., pp. 351, 354, emphasis added.
52. cf. transcript, The Ankerberg Theological Research Institute, *Is Abortion Justifiable?*
53. Curt Young, *The Least of These: What Everyone Should Know About Abortion* (Chicago, IL: Moody Press, 1984), p 85.
54. Exley, p. 43.
55. Transcript, The Ankerberg Theological Research Institute, *Is Abortion Justifiable?*, p. 4.
56. Young, p. 85.
57. Ibid., pp. 87-88.
58. Young, p. 96.
59. Ibid. p. 89.
60. Ibid.
61. Ibid., p. 95.
62. Hilgers and Horan, p. 77.
63. Shettles, *Rites of Life: The Scientific Evidence for Life Before Birth*, p. 116.
64. "Abortion: Hard Questions and Elusive Answers," *USA Today*, April 24, 1984.

65. Hilgers, Horan and Mall (eds.), p. 213.
66. Transcript, The Ankerberg Theological Research Institute, *Is Abortion Justifiable?*, p. 5.
67. Hilgers, Horan and Mall (eds.), pp. 212-13.
68. Ibid., p. 213.
69. James K. Hoffmeier, (ed.) *Abortion: A Christian Understanding and Response* (Grand Rapids, MI: Baker, 1987), pp. 167-68, see 144.
70. Exley, p. 56.
71. Reardon, pp. xvi-xix.
72. Hilgers and Horan, pp. 58, 77.
73. For detailed documentation see note 75, John Ankerberg and John Weldon, *When Does Life Begin?* (1989), footnotes 57-58, 82-83.
74. Debra Evans, *Without Moral Limits: Women, Reproduction and the New Medical Technology* (Westchester, IL: Crossway Books, 1989), pp. 60-61.
75. See note 73 and Wanda Franz, Testimony, U.S. Congress, House, Human Resources and Intergovernmental Relations Subcommittee of the Committee on Government Operations, Hearing on *Medical and Psychological Impact of Abortion*, 101st Cong., First Session, Mar. 16, 1989. See also Vincent Rue, *The Hatch Hearings*, vol. 1, pp. 329-78; N. Spreckhard, *The Psycho-Social Stress Following Abortion* (Kansas City, MO: Sheed and Ward, 1987); N. Spreckhard (ed.), *Post Abortion Trauma* (1987); David Mall and Walter F. Watts, M.D. (ed.), *Psychological Aspects of Abortion*, Frederick, MD, University Publications of America, 1979; The Rutherford Institute, *Major Articles and Books Concerning the Detrimental Effects of Abortion* (summary report from hundreds of scientific studies published in medical and psychological journals), Manassas, VA (P.O. Box 510), The Rutherford Institute.
76. National Right to Life Educational Trust Fund, "Abortion: Some Medical Facts," Washington, D.C., NRLETF, 1989, p. 5.
77. Reardon, p. 93.
78. Ibid., p. 96, cf. *Bernadell Technical Bulletin*, Nov. 1989 (see ref. *Christianity Today*, July 14, 1989).
79. Ibid., p. 97.
80. Ibid., p. 99.
81. Ibid., pp. 100-01.
82. Reardon, pp. 109-11.
83. Ibid., p. 119.
84. Fowler, p. 196.
85. Interview with Coleman McCarthy, "Does Abortion Harden Maternal Instinct?," *National Catholic Reporter*, Feb. 24, 1989, p. 20.
86. Vincent M. Rue, et al., *A Report on the Psychological Aftermath of Abortion*, p. 53.
87. Reardon, pp. 119-20.
88. Ibid., p. 129.
89. Ibid., pp. 130-31.
90. See note 73.
91. Rue, et al., *A Report on the Psychological Aftermath of Abortion*, p. 4.
92. National Right to Life Educational Trust Fund, "Abortion: Some Medical Facts," Washington, D.C., NRLETF, 1989, p. 7.
93. Ibid., p. 5.
94. Rue, et al., *A Report on the Psychological Aftermath of Abortion*.
95. Ibid., p. 8.
96. Ibid., p. 7.
97. Ibid., pp. 6-7.
98. Ibid., p. 53.
99. Ibid., p. 54.

100. P. Ney, "A Consideration of Abortion Survivors," *Child Psychiatry and Human Development*, vol. 13, 1982, pp. 168-79.
101. Fowler, p. 147.
102. Herbert T. Krimmel and Martin J. Foley, "Abortion and Human Life: A Christian Perspective" *The Simon Greenleaf Law Review*, vol. 5 (1985-86), pp. 12-13.
103. Umberto Cassuto, *Commentary on the Book of Exodus* (Jerusalem: Magnes Press, The Hebrew University, 1967), p. 275.
104. C. F. Keil, F. Delitzsch, *Commentary on the Old Testament in Ten Volumes*, vol. 1 (Exodus) (Grand Rapids, MI: Eerdmans, 1978), pp. 134-35.
105. Television program transcript, "Abortion," Chattanooga, TN, The John Ankerberg Evangelistic Association, 1982, p. 3.
106. James F. Humber, Robert F. Almeder, *Biomedical Ethics and the Law* (NewYork: Plenum Press, 1976), pp. 72, 84.